my itty-bitty bio

Cesar Chavez

CHERRY LAKE PRESS

Published in the United States of America by Cherry Lake Publishing
Ann Arbor, Michigan
www.cherrylakepublishing.com

Reading Adviser: Beth Walker Gambro, MS, Ed., Reading Consultant, Yorkville, IL
Illustrator: Leo Trinidad

Photo Credits: © Berns Images / Shutterstock, 5; Library of Congress, 7, 9, 11, 22; PH3 BRYANT / US NAVY Defense Visual Information Center via Wikimedia Commons, public domain, 13; Los Angeles Daily News / UCLA via Wikimedia Commons CC-BY 4.0, 15; Bibliothèque nationale de France, département Estampes et photographie, EI-13(2866) via Wikimedia Commons, public domain, 17; © ASSOCIATED PRESS, 19, 23; © ZUMA Press, Inc. / Alamy Stock Photo, 21

Copyright © 2025 by Cherry Lake Publishing
All rights reserved. No part of this book may be reproduced or utilized in
any form or by any means without written permission from the publisher.

Cherry Lake Press is an imprint of Cherry Lake Publishing Group

Library of Congress Cataloging-in-Publication Data has been filed and is available
at catalog.loc.gov.

Printed in the United States of America

table of contents

My Story 4

Timeline 22

Glossary 24

Index 24

About the author: Brenda Perez Mendoza is an award-winning educator and the author of the Racial Justice in America: Latinx American series. She grew up in Cicero, Illinois, as a native language Spanish speaker. When she went to school, there wasn't enough support for students learning the English language. That is what drove her to become a K–12 ELL specialist and work with bilingual students. She works to advocate for all students, Latinx especially, to embrace their culture and celebrate who they are. Today, she lives in Chicago, Illinois, and is committed to providing students with culturally responsive practices and advocating for the whole child.

About the illustrator: Leo Trinidad is a NY Times bestselling comic book artist, illustrator, and animator from Costa Rica. For more than 12 years he's been creating content for children's books and TV shows. Leo created the first animated series ever produced in Central America, and founded Rocket Cartoons, one of the most successful animation studios in Latin America. He is also the 2018 winner of the Central American Graphic Novel contest.

my story

I was born in Arizona in 1927. My family owned a farm there.

I am Mexican American.

We had to sell our farm. It was the **Great Depression**.

Times were hard.

We moved to California. I was 11 years old. We lived in a place called Sal Si Puedes.

It means "get out if you can."

I worked in the fields. I had to help earn money. I went to school. But I spoke only Spanish.

My school banned the Spanish language.

What language do you speak at home?

I joined the U.S. Navy. I was 19. The Navy was **segregated**.

It was not fair.

We moved to Delano, California. I was a farm worker. Farm workers worked hard. We were very poor. We were not treated well.

I wanted to change things.

What would you change?

I read about Mahatma Gandhi. He was a leader in India. I learned about **nonviolence**.

I wanted to make lives better.

I worked for my community. I helped form the United Farm Workers.

I fought for equal rights. I led marches. I led **boycotts**.

I was a civil rights leader. I died in 1993. My legacy lives on.

I still inspire people.

What would you like to ask me?

timeline

1938

1900

Born
1927

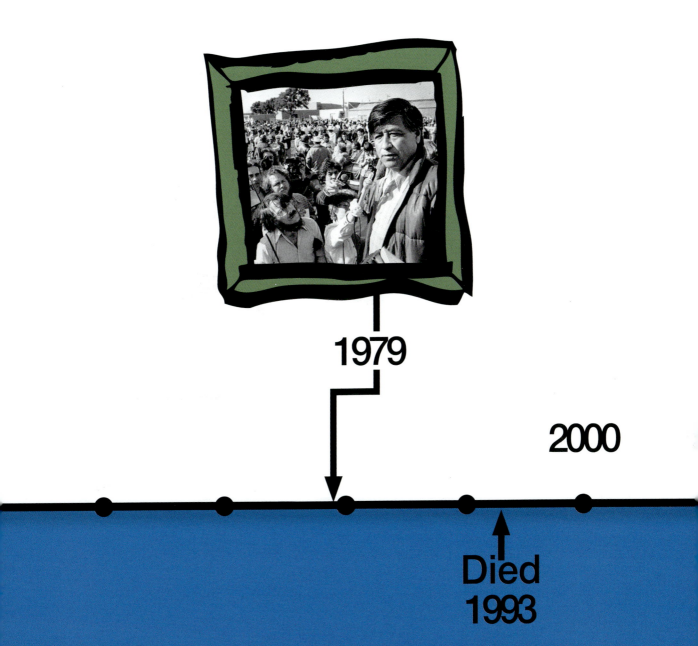

glossary & index

glossary

boycotts (BOY-kahts) protests where people refuse to buy a good or use a service

Great Depression (GRAYT dih-PREH-shuhn) a time in the 1930s when many people lost jobs and had little money

nonviolence (nahn-VIE-uh-luhns) a way to cause political change without using violence

segregated (SEH-grih-gay-tuhd) separated based on race and treated unfairly

index

activism, 14, 16–20
Arizona, 4

birth, 4, 22

California, 8, 14

death, 20, 23

education, 10

farm workers, 4–7, 10–11, 14–15, 18–19

Gandhi, Mohandas K., 16–17
Great Depression, 6–7

labor rights, 14–15, 16, 18–19

nonviolent resistance, 16–20

segregation, 12
Spanish language, 10

timeline, 22–23

U.S. Navy, 12–13
United Farm Workers (UFW), 18–19